TRAPPED

Other books by George Sullivan
you will enjoy:

Not Guilty: Five Times When Justice Failed

Alamo!

In the Line of Fire: Eight Women War Spies

The Day the Women Got the Vote

TRAPPED

George Sullivan

Scholastic Inc.
New York Toronto London Auckland Sydney

Cover photo of Jessica McClure: Wide World

No part of this publication may be reproduced in whole or in part, or stored in a retrieval system, or transmitted in any form or by any means, electronic, mechanical, photocopying, recording, or otherwise, without written permission of the publisher. For information regarding permission, write to Scholastic Inc., Attention: Permissions Department, 555 Broadway, New York, NY 10012.

ISBN 0-590-29894-1

12 11 10 9 8 7 6 5 4 3 2 1   8 9/9 0 1 2/0

Printed in the U.S.A.   40
First Scholastic printing, February 1998

Contents

TRAPPED

Introduction

Caves always fascinated Floyd Collins. He liked caves the way some people like flowers or birds.

Once, while chasing a woodchuck near his home in Cave City, Kentucky, Collins discovered a cavern of stunning beauty. It became known as Crystal Cave for its "myriad white gypsum flowers," and would one day develop into a popular tourist attraction.

Early one morning in January 1925, Collins decided to investigate a sand hole he had found to see whether it led to a cave. Beyond the mouth of the hole was a dark, damp, sloping passage. Floyd crawled into it, then wriggled along on his belly like a snake.

As the incline got steeper, Floyd slid along in the darkness, slowing only for twists and turns in the passageway. Eventually the dark, wet cavern ended, and Floyd looked out upon what he later would call "the most beautiful cave he had ever seen in his life."

But before Floyd could report his discovery to the outside world, disaster struck. As he started crawling out of the cave, he knocked loose a huge chunk of limestone, which fell on his left leg, pinning his foot in a crevice. Floyd tried everything, but he could not free himself. In fact, his movements caused more stones to pile up.

Floyd spent the night in the cave calling for help. He also did a lot of praying.

The next morning, when Floyd was nowhere to be found, a friend crawled into the mouth of the cavern and shouted out his name. Floyd answered from far below, saying he was trapped. The friend went for help.

Soon after, Floyd's brother, Homer, crawled through the blackness of the cave until he came to Floyd. He was lying on his left side, his left leg still trapped by the massive block of limestone. Homer tried to free his brother, but he could not.

Homer crawled back out and later returned with food for Floyd. He also carried burlap sacks, which he placed over his brother to keep him warm. He put strips of burlap over Floyd's head to shield him from water that was dripping in his face.

The first rescuers to arrive upon the scene carried a harness into the cave. They put the harness around Floyd's body and tried to pull him free, but Floyd's body wouldn't move an inch.

Within a few days, the crisis surrounding Floyd Collins had caught the attention of the entire country. Newspaper reporters flocked to the site. People stayed close to their radios for the latest news of Floyd. (This was before television.)

Hundreds of rescuers worked day and night in an effort to reach Floyd, who had become weakened by pain. They first tried to widen the entrance to the cave so that rescue equipment could be hauled through it. In the midst of their efforts, the passageway caved in, blocking access to Floyd.

It was then decided to sink a new shaft from the surface. Because of the fear of causing another cave-in and perhaps burying poor Floyd, heavy machinery could not be used. Workers dug with picks and shovels.

On the second Sunday in February, special prayers were said for Floyd in cities and towns throughout the United States. Floyd had now been trapped for nine days. Speaking from the White House, President Calvin Coolidge expressed his hope and sympathy.

That week, rain began falling. The sand turned into muck, slowing the digging.

Tests made with a microphone and radio amplifier gave evidence that Floyd was still alive, even though he had been without food for about a week.

But hope was fading. Finally, on February 16, some two and a half weeks after Floyd had entered the cave, diggers reached a point only a few feet from where he lay. Rescue workers then tunneled into the cave that had become Floyd's prison.

One of the rescuers entered the cave. All was silent for a moment. Then the man backed out and quietly said one word: "Dead."

Funeral services were held for Floyd not far from the sand hole where he had entered the cave, and then the cave was sealed. His body was later removed and placed in a casket in Crystal Cave, the cavern he had discovered a few years before.

If the rock that had trapped Floyd Collins had snuffed out his life instantly, the tragedy would have earned a line or two in the newspapers and then have been forgotten. Surely, Floyd Collins would never have become famous.

But accounts of people who are trapped have a power all their own. They command both wonder and horror from us.

Six stories of people trapped, their lives in peril, are presented in this book. The stories tell of sailors trapped in a submarine at the bottom of the ocean and brave mountain climbers caught in a fierce storm on the slopes of Mount Everest, the highest mountain on Earth. They tell of men trapped almost a mile below the surface in the tunnel of a silver mine and of young children stuck in an elevator in one of the twin towers of the World Trade Center.

Like the tale of Floyd Collins, they are stories of courage and daring. They can also be stories of death-dealing mistakes and remarkable rescues.

And central to them all is a burning desire to stay alive.

As evidence, there is the case of 29-year-old Tom Wilkinson, who was trapped in the silence and inky blackness of an Idaho silver mine for eight days. Years later, he was asked to recall his most vivid memory of that experience. Wilkinson shook his head and grinned. "Getting out," he said.

• 1 •

Ordeal in a Well

During the second week of October 1987, Americans were served up a big helping of disturbing news. From the White House came an announcement that Nancy Reagan, the First Lady, found to be suffering from breast cancer, was to undergo surgery. "I guess it's my turn," said a saddened Mrs. Reagan.

In the Persian Gulf, Iran launched a missile that hit a Kuwaiti oil tanker flying the American flag.

In New York City, the stock market experienced a record one-day drop that sent shock waves around the world.

For the most part, however, these stories were nudged into the background, never getting the attention that they otherwise might have deserved.

That's because people everywhere were caught up in a crisis surrounding little Jessica McClure of

1

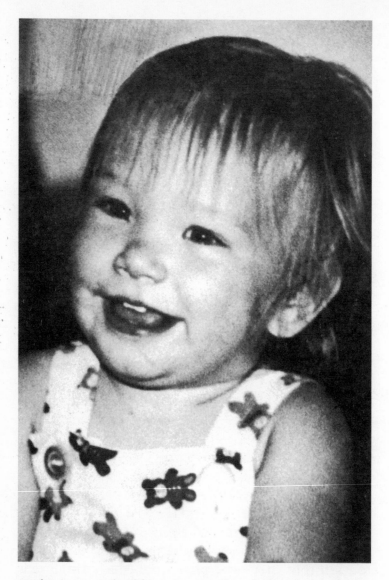

Eighteen-month-old Jessica McClure before her ordeal in the well. (Wide World)

Midland, Texas. Jessica fell down a dark, narrow abandoned well and was trapped underground for more than two days. Jessica's story captured the heart of the nation.

People kept the television on for news bulletins about Jessica. They stayed tuned to the all-news stations on their car radios and got up early to buy the latest newspapers.

"All across the world people were watching this thing in Midland, Texas, and if they didn't get tears in their eyes, they're not human," said James Shaw, one of the workers who toiled day and night in an effort to rescue Jessica. "I know there were tears in my eyes. I'm not afraid to tell you that."

Jessica's dramatic tale began not long before ten o'clock in the morning on Wednesday, October 14. The 18-month-old toddler was playing with other children about her age in the backyard of a day care center, which was run by Jessica's aunt. Jessica's mother, 17-year-old Reba (Cissy) McClure, helped out there. Jessica's father, Chip McClure, 18 years old, a housepainter, was at work.

Mrs. McClure had gone into the house for a moment when she heard the children in the backyard screaming. Somehow Jessica had fallen down an abandoned well shaft.

No one knows exactly how it happened. The opening to the well, about the size of a dinner plate, had been covered, either by a flowerpot or a heavy rock.

3

While only about eight inches wide at the top, the well got wider farther down. Then it narrowed again, closing to a diameter of about six inches. Jessica came to rest many feet from the top, just above the spot where the shaft started getting narrower.

When Mrs. McClure discovered what had happened, she ran into the house and called the police. A police car and ambulance arrived at the house within a few minutes.

"She's here in back!" Mrs. McClure cried out to B. J. Hall, the first police officer to arrive. "She fell down here in back!"

Taking a flashlight, Officer Hall looked down the hole but couldn't see anything. Mrs. McClure bent over the hole beside him. She couldn't see anything either.

Then the officer called out Jessica's name several times. There was no response.

Officer Hall kept calling Jessica's name down the hole. Finally, he and Mrs. McClure heard a faint cry.

"We gotta get some air down there," Hall said to a fellow officer. He radioed police headquarters and ordered oxygen equipment.

News of what had happened spread quickly throughout Midland, a city of about 100,000 in the heart of the oil fields of West Texas. Soon the backyard began filling up with neighbors and rescue workers.

Various kinds of rescue equipment also kept arriving. Drivers tore down clotheslines and overran fences in their haste to get to the scene.

Rescue workers attached a flashlight to a tape measure and lowered it into the hole. When it stopped unreeling, the tape measure read almost 22 feet.

Workers also lowered a microphone and small speaker into the hole so that they could talk to Jessica. "The only thing I heard her say is 'Mommy,'" a police officer reported. "The rest is just crying or moaning."

Rather than try to pull Jessica from the well, workers decided the best way to rescue her was to dig a second shaft parallel to the well. When the rescue shaft had reached Jessica's level, they would tunnel horizontally into the well casing and bring her out.

Workers began excavating with a backhoe, a machine that digs up great scoops of earth with each bite. But after three or four feet, the backhoe hit solid rock and stopped making progress.

Then a "rat-holer," a type of drill used to bore holes for telephone poles, was brought in. The towering rig looked out of place in the backyard of the small frame house.

Meanwhile, as television and radio stations began carrying accounts of the rescue efforts, the switchboard at Midland's police headquarters was jammed with callers. Two people normally answered the telephones. But a dozen were needed as people around the world became concerned about Jessica. Calls came in not only from virtually every state in the United States, but from Canada, Mexico, and "even Australia," a police lieutenant reported.

Some people offered help. Others merely wanted up-to-date information about attempts to rescue Jessica.

As the drilling continued, workers kept calling out words of encouragement to Jessica. Sometimes they sang nursery rhymes to her. At one point, she sang along with "Humpty Dumpty."

Humpty Dumpty sat on a wall.
Humpty Dumpty had a great fall.
All the king's horses and all the king's men
Couldn't put Humpty together again.

Another time, Jessica sang "Winnie the Pooh."

Workers often tried to engage Jessica in conversation. "How does a kitten go?" a worker would say. "Meow, meow," Jessica would answer.

Jessica's parents spent most of the day inside. Jessica's father, Chip McClure, came out and spoke briefly to newspaper and television reporters. He thanked the companies that had donated equipment and the many volunteers who had given their time. "With the Lord's help and your prayers, this little girl is going to make it," he said.

The rescue efforts continued through the afternoon and into the evening. At nightfall, city workers set up floodlights. Rescuers set up a hose that carried warm air to Jessica.

The little girl dozed on and off throughout the night. She also cried. The drilling stopped only for short periods so that Jessica's mother could talk to her daughter down the shaft.

By the next day, Thursday, the scene at the surface looked like a war zone. Local police and firefighters had arrived at the scene shortly after they were notified of Jessica's plight. They were joined by scores of paramedics, oil-field technicians, Red Cross workers, sheriff's deputies, and volunteers. The din of air compressors made conversation difficult.

Although Jessica's crying had stopped, rescue workers could tell that she was still alive by means of a supersensitive microphone that had been lowered into the well. It picked up sounds of her moving and breathing.

And all across the nation, people stayed glued to their television screens for news from the rescue scene.

David Lilly, a special investigator with the U.S. Mine Safety and Health Administration, was one of the experts to arrive on Thursday. By the time Lilly got to Midland, workers had already drilled a rescue shaft about 29 feet deep and 30 inches wide and just a few feet from the shaft that held Jessica.

The next step was to drill a horizontal tunnel, about five feet long, that would connect the rescue shaft and the well. Lilly suggested that they change the angle at which they planned to drill so that they would break through at a point below where Jessica was trapped. The drill could hit Jessica if they punched through the well pipe right where Jessica was stuck.

But there was a problem. The solid bone-colored rock was much harder than anyone had expected it to be. It kept wearing down the drill bits after just a few inches of drilling. Then the bits would have to be hauled to the surface and sharpened. Lilly was able to acquire bits made of tungsten carbide, which lasted longer.

In cutting the passageway that was to link the two shafts, the workers' strategy was to first drill a series of holes a few inches apart through the rock. Once a number of holes had been drilled, they would use a jackhammer to knock out the remaining rock.

It was tough going. The man operating the jackhammer had to lie on his stomach, holding the 45-pound machine in front of him. Choking rock dust threatened to suffocate the workers, and the jackhammer's high-pitched clatter pierced their eardrums. One man passed out from exhaustion and had to be hauled to the top of the shaft for treatment.

As rescue workers got closer to the well casing, they switched from jackhammers to a hydro drill, which spurted a jet of water that generated a force of about 40,000 pounds per square inch. Workers believed the hydro drill would speed up the work.

Even with the hydro drill, it was Friday morning before drillers reached the well casing that held Jessica. Lilly himself was manning the hydro drill when it broke through into the shaft. He set aside the drill, reached up, and felt Jessica's foot and leg. Jessica started crying.

During the two days she had been in the well, Jessica had slipped down the pipe several more inches. Lilly inserted a metal rod through the pipe below where Jessica was stuck to prevent her from slipping any farther. And he also placed a heavy industrial balloon in the pipe beneath her to

Jessica's mother, Reba McClure (foreground), waits anxiously while rescue workers seek to reach her daughter.
(Wide World)

protect Jessica from the dust and shield her from the noise made by drillers as they sought to increase the size of the shaft.

Once the drilling was completed, the workers were brought to the surface. Paramedics replaced them.

Mrs. McClure came outside to watch. She was clutching a yellow teddy bear that she wanted to give to Jessica.

Thirty-year-old Robert O'Donnell was the first paramedic to make contact with Jessica. Early Friday afternoon, O'Donnell got into a harness connected to a cable, switched on his miner's light, and then was lowered slowly down the rescue shaft. By this time, Jessica had been in the well more than 50 hours.

Once he entered the tunnel connecting the two shafts, O'Donnell squirmed his way along on his belly. When he reached the opening in the well casing, poked his head through, and looked up, he could see Jessica's left foot dangling.

Jessica's mother had told O'Donnell that Jessica's nickname was Juicy. "Move your foot for me, Juicy," O'Donnell said. Jessica swung her foot.

Not only did O'Donnell want to learn as much as he could about Jessica's physical condition, he wanted to find out the position of her body. Was she in a seated position? Was she lying down?

But about all that O'Donnell was able to establish was that Jessica was firmly stuck in the pipe.

She could not, or would not, move in one direction or the other.

O'Donnell thought about tugging hard at Jessica, trying to pull her toward him. But he decided against doing so, afraid that he might break her back or neck.

O'Donnell returned to the surface to explain to Dave Lilly that he needed more room in order to be able to get closer to Jessica. Lilly sent the drillers back down the rescue shaft to enlarge the tunnel leading to the well casing. The job took several hours.

When O'Donnell went back down the shaft and worked his way through the tunnel and into the well casing to the point where Jessica was stuck, he was able to determine what the problem was: Jessica was sitting in the pipe with her left leg hanging straight down, but her right leg was stretched upward so her foot was up by her head. "She was in a split," O'Donnell reported, and her forehead was pressed against the wall of the well.

O'Donnell decided that he had no choice but to try to pull Jessica out. But before he began pulling, he coated the inside walls of the pipe with petroleum jelly from a container that he had brought with him. Maybe this would help to slide her out, he thought.

When O'Donnell reached with one hand and grasped Jessica's thigh and began pulling, the little girl screamed. O'Donnell, calling her Juicy, tried to calm her. "Everything's going to be all right, Juicy," he said. But Jessica would not stop screaming.

O'Donnell kept pulling. "No!" Jessica cried out at one point. But O'Donnell would not stop. When one arm got tired, he pulled with the other.

O'Donnell breathed a sigh of relief when he noticed that he had moved Jessica a couple of inches. When her body entered the section that had been coated with petroleum jelly, she moved even more. Now she was moving an inch or more each time he pulled.

With one final tug, O'Donnell pulled Jessica out of the well casing and into the tunnel leading to the rescue shaft. Caked with dirt, resting on her back, Jessica stared up at O'Donnell, blinked her eyes, and looked around.

"You're out, Juicy," O'Donnell said with a grin. "You're out."

Behind O'Donnell in the tunnel was a second paramedic, Steve Forbes. He carried a specially made board with him, which he passed to O'Donnell. The paramedic placed Jessica on the board.

With Jessica in position, O'Donnell pushed the board back between his legs to Forbes, who strapped her down. Both men wriggled their way back to the rescue shaft. Workers at the surface had lowered the cable and Forbes hitched his harness to it. He held Jessica in his arms so that she faced him as the pair was slowly hoisted up.

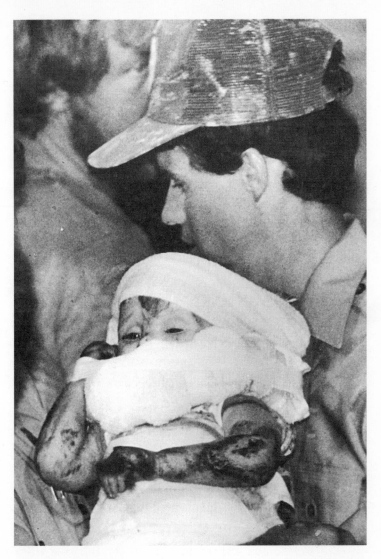

A firefighter carries Jessica to a waiting ambulance after she had been brought to the surface. (Wide World)

As their heads poked above the surface, Jessica and Forbes were greeted with a burst of loud cheers and applause from the crowd. Many people sobbed with joy. Dozens of car horns blared and firecrackers exploded all over town. Jessica's mother rushed up to hug and kiss her daughter.

Once it was known that Jessica's ordeal was coming to an end, all three television networks interrupted their regular programming to report the good news. CNN carried a continuous stream of updates.

A waiting ambulance whisked Jessica and her parents to Midland Memorial Hospital. The streets of the city were lined with people, and as the ambulance passed they yelled and cheered.

That night, as doctors examined Jessica in the hospital emergency room, a parade of cars circled the hospital. The switchboard was overwhelmed with calls from well-wishers around the world.

Doctors who examined Jessica found her to be in generally good health, with no broken bones or internal injuries. However, she had a bruise on her forehead and her right foot was swollen and badly bruised and suffered from a lack of circulation. (Later, two toes from Jessica's right foot would have to be amputated.)

During the 58½ hours she spent in the well, Jessica's weight had dropped from 21 pounds to 17½ pounds and she was found to be dehydrated. Liq-

Her right foot in a cast, Jessica walks with her mother after being released from the hospital. (Wide World)

uids were pumped into her body and she was given solid food.

"The mother's been up there hugging and kissing her," one of the doctors told the news media. "What this baby needs is for her mother to hold her — and that's what she's doing."

As doctors and nurses attended Jessica, hospital volunteers were called upon to make room for the great flood of gifts that had started to pour in. More than a thousand balloons, flower arrangements, and stuffed toy animals were received at the hospital within a few hours after Jessica's arrival.

The next day, President Ronald Reagan and his wife, Nancy, who was recovering from surgery for breast cancer, called from the First Lady's hospital room. They offered their best wishes to Jessica's parents.

In their telephone conversation with the Reagans, and at a news conference that day, Jessica's parents said that they were trying to figure out a way to thank the hundreds of rescue workers who had labored night and day to save their daughter.

"I'm so glad we got her back safe," said Jessica's mother. "The whole world has her back."

Two weeks after Jessica's rescue, the city of Midland held a parade for the more than 400 men and women who worked to rescue Jessica. The little girl watched the parade from her hospital window.

Three weeks later, her right foot still in a cast, Jessica was released from the hospital.

The well shaft in which Jessica was trapped was later filled with concrete, then capped with a metal cover bearing the message:

FOR JESSICA, 10-16-87, WITH LOVE FROM ALL OF US.

Today, Jessica has no memory of her ordeal. The incident that gripped the entire nation has been forgotten by its central figure.

· 2 ·

Fire Below!

Hard-rock metal mining is a tough life. The darkness within the mines is like a cloak over one's head. The heat gets so intense, soaring to over 100 degrees, that even strong men can be stricken with cramps. The constant *rat-a-tat-tat* of heavy steel drills pierces the ears, while years of breathing rock dust rots the lungs.

It was like that at the Sunshine Mine, the nation's deepest and richest silver mine. Discovered in 1884, the Sunshine Mine is one of about two dozen hard-rock mines strewn from east to west along Interstate 90 through the rugged hills of northern Idaho.

Mining is a way of life in the area. "After you're seventeen, they start hiring you, and people quit school and come out here and work," a high school junior once explained. "It's the only way they can make enough money to get a car. They have to get into town for the parties and the dances, and they can't always get their dad's car."

Besides the rugged working conditions, miners have to learn to live with the threat of injury and death. Year in and year out, men die from rock falls, accidents involving mine equipment, or falls down mine shafts. Between 1966 and 1970, 24 men died in the hard-rock metal mines of northern Idaho, five of them in the Sunshine Mine.

Despite a less than glowing safety record, no one was prepared for the disaster that struck the Sunshine Mine late on the morning of May 2, 1972.

The fateful May day began like most others, with no hint of the disaster to come. At seven o'clock in the morning, the day's workforce of 201 miners and support personnel assembled at the Jewell shaft to be taken to their workstations below.

The elevator, or cage, as the miners called it, carried 48 men at a time. It took about 20 minutes to transport the work crew to the mine's 3,700-foot level.

Besides being the site of the shaft elevator station, the 3,700-foot level housed the underground foreman's office and several small maintenance shops — the pipe, electric, and machine shops.

At the 3,700-foot level, the miners boarded the open railroad cars that made up what they called a man train. The train carried them through a mile-long tunnel, or drift, to the No. 10 shaft, a long, narrow, vertical passage. There they boarded a second cage that took them to the lower working levels — at 4,200 feet, 4,800 feet, 5,200 feet, and 5,600 feet.

Hard-rock miners at the Sunshine Mine often worked in a cycle in which each day ended with blasting. As the miners' shift began, they found piles of blasted rock in the drifts. Working in pairs, they knocked down any loose rock from the roof and sides of the blasted area. Then they wet down the crushed rock and slushed out, that is, scooped up, the wet rock with mechanical buckets and hauled it to an ore car.

The final hours of the shift were spent drilling deep holes into the rock. Each hole was filled with a charge of dynamite that was exploded. When they finished blasting, the miners went home.

Bob McCoy, 56 years old, tall and thin, a miner for 30 years, worked as a timber repairman in the mine. On May 2, McCoy was assigned to work at the 5,200-foot level. He finished eating lunch, closed up his lunch bucket, and checked his watch. It was 11:30 A.M., time to go back to work.

Not long after, while repairing timber supports at the hoist station of the No. 10 shaft, McCoy noticed smoke billowing down the shaft from above. It came swirling toward him, poisoning the air. Other miners who had smelled the smoke began gathering at the hoist station.

"There's fire up there," someone shouted.

These are scary words in an underground mine. Even the smallest blaze, a fire in an oil drum, for example, is a fearful matter.

Smoke and carbon monoxide generated by the flames can quickly poison the air. A miner can be overcome by carbon monoxide in a matter of seconds. Death can quickly follow.

Before long, there were about 20 miners waiting at the hoist station. They kept peering up the shaft, looking for the cage that would haul them to safety. They waited and waited, but the cage did not come.

Someone handed out self-rescuers from a supply kept in a storage chest at the hoist station. The self-rescuer, a breathing device that looks like a gas mask, converts poisonous carbon monoxide gas into breathable carbon dioxide.

As more and more smoke poured down the shaft, the men retreated into the tunnel. There they opened a compressed-air line, meant to supply air to power mine machinery. But the sudden flow of air from the open line didn't help very much.

After about half an hour of waiting, the cage arrived. By that time, many of the men were so weak that they had to be pushed into the cage. Although the cage was tightly packed when it departed, about half of the waiting men, including McCoy, had to be left behind.

When the cage returned, McCoy and the others crowded aboard. McCoy felt okay at the time. He felt so good, in fact, that he left his self-rescuer behind in case someone else coming out of the tunnel might need it.

At the 3,700-foot level, McCoy and the others left the cage. Since there was no man train waiting, they started walking toward the Jewell shaft. They had gone only a few hundred feet when McCoy felt too weak to go any farther. He slumped to the ground, then sat with his chin on his chest at the side of the tunnel. Within minutes, he was unconscious. When the man train arrived, McCoy had to be lifted aboard.

Ron Flory, 28 years old, and Tom Wilkinson, 29, were working together at the 4,800-foot level when the fire broke out. At the first whiff of smoke, Flory and Wilkinson and seven other miners raced for the shaft station to wait for the cage that would take them back to the 3,700-foot level. But the cage never showed up. Worse, smoke kept sweeping down the shaft, threatening to smother them.

Flory and Wilkinson turned and ran farther into the tunnel until they found good air from compressed-air lines. The seven other miners trailed after them, but smoke and deadly carbon monoxide gas enveloped the seven before they could reach safety. All collapsed, unconscious.

Wilkinson nearly passed out, too. He stumbled and fell as he sought to escape. Flory dragged him into the fresh air of the tunnel.

Once the two men realized they were safe, Flory returned to look for the other miners. They were all dead. Flory hurried back to the tunnel where he had left Wilkinson, and the two men began a long wait.

Flory and Wilkinson were two of 93 men trapped in the mine's vast honeycomb of tunnels. Some 108 miners had been able to escape.

Mine officials believed that the fire must have started in one of the mine's old workings, an abandoned tunnel that had been sealed off from the rest of the mine. Such tunnels were often filled with old, dry timbers used to support tunnel roofs and walls.

Fire could start in such timbers through spontaneous combustion, the heat increasing naturally within the wood until it reached a flash point.

Other mine-safety experts thought the fire had been caused by a short circuit in the electrical system in an unused part of the mine, and that it burned for some time without being detected.

Whatever the cause, around 11:30 A.M. a miner heard an explosion. Experts said it was probably the sound of the fire bursting through the barricade that was meant to close off that section of the mine.

Within minutes after the explosion, a deadly combination of smoke and carbon monoxide filtered into the mine's ventilation system and spread quickly.

Wives, children, and other relatives of the missing hurried to the mine. They stood in small groups or sat in folding chairs within a roped-off area near the mine entrance. Some women sobbed.

At mine headquarters, relatives and friends of trapped miners await word from rescue workers.
(Spokane Spokesman Review)

More than a hundred local men took part in the effort to rescue the missing men. They were joined by a dozen experts from the Federal Bureau of Mines.

Rescue workers pumped clean air into the ventilation system, hoping to force the bad air out. However, white smoke continued to pour from the mine exhaust pipe, evidence that the fire was still burning below.

The Sunshine Mine had two main escape tunnels. Directions to each of them were posted in the mine.

But mine officials pointed out that the routes to the tunnels were blocked by smoke once the fire started. The chances for a worker to escape through one of the tunnels were described as being "very, very slim."

Four-man rescue teams wearing self-rescuers entered the mine to search for survivors. They slowly made their way through the dark tunnels, lighting them with their headlights.

Their goal was to reach the elevator in the No. 10 shaft, about a mile from the mine's main entrance. That elevator was the only means of getting to the mine's lower reaches, where many workers were believed to be trapped.

Within two days after the fire broke out, 24 bodies had been discovered in the mine's smoke-choked tunnels. The next day, eight more bodies were found. Still missing were 61 men.

Rescuers hoped that some of the missing men had survived by seeking out remote corners of the

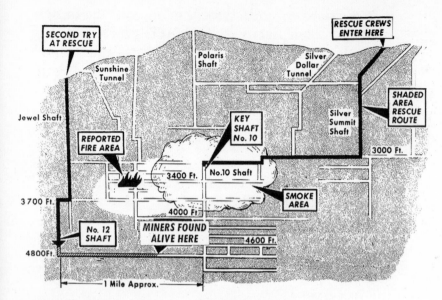

Mine shafts within the Sunshine Mine penetrated to more than a mile below the surface. (Wide World)

mine. There they could breathe air provided by the compressed-air system.

But Marvin Chase, the mine's general manager, did not appear hopeful, saying that a mine such as the Sunshine was not well equipped to handle an underground fire. "All of the mines in this district are sixty to seventy years old," he said. "There are hundreds of old workings and myriad openings that smoke can seep through. It's a very difficult job in a mine this old."

Nearly a mile underground, Ron Flory and Tom Wilkinson huddled together in a silent underground passage.

Before the first day had ended, the lights on their miner's hats burned out. Now they sat alone in the dark. They were heartened by the fact that the smoke and deadly carbon monoxide gas began to be replaced by fresh air being pumped in from above.

To pass the long hours, the two men braided blasting wires.

"We prayed a lot and we talked a lot," Wilkinson was to recall later. "We talked about fishing and hunting. We talked about cars.

"We didn't know how bad it was; we didn't know how many men had died or how many men were still trapped. We thought we might be the only ones.

"We knew that they must be doing something to try and find us. We figured all we had to do was keep waiting."

Food was not a big problem. Once the air had cleared somewhat and they could move around, Flory and Wilkinson discovered the lunch pails of the seven men who had died. They remained just where the owners had placed them when their shift began.

As the days passed, Flory and Wilkinson ate the lunches. For liquid, they drank water from a cooling line that ran through the tunnel in which they had taken shelter.

At the surface, Ron Flory's 18-year-old wife, Myrna, was one of hundreds who waited for word about the trapped miners. A smallish, freckle-faced woman, and the mother of a two-year-old son, Mrs. Flory told a reporter for *The New York Times,* "I don't want to become a widow at eighteen."

Clergymen had asked family members of the miners to wear name tags so that each person could be located quickly should news come. But Mrs. Flory refused to wear a tag with her husband's name written on it. She was afraid that a clergyman might walk up to her and tell her that her husband was dead. "I only want them to tell me if he's alive," she said.

Hope for the trapped men waned when a huge cave-in cut the lines carrying compressed air to the mine's lower levels. Earlier, the system had sprung a leak, and the air pressure had dropped to one-third of what it was normally.

The fire continued to burn, resisting all efforts to seal it off and smother it.

One chance remained for rescuing those who might still be alive. The Federal Bureau of Mines shipped a torpedolike capsule to the scene. Yellow in color, the capsule was seven feet long and almost four feet in diameter. The idea was to attach the capsule to a strong cable and lower it and its two-man crew down an air shaft.

They would descend to various levels within the mine, allowing the two crew members to leave the capsule to search for survivors. They would carry a portable breathing apparatus with them.

Six days after the fire had broken out, all was ready. The two experts from the Federal Bureau

With room enough for two crew members, this cylindrical capsule was lowered down an airshaft in a last-ditch rescue attempt. (Spokane Spokesman Review)

of Mines entered the capsule at the 3,700-foot level, prepared to be lowered another 1,100 feet. Since the air shaft was only four feet across, it was a tight fit for the capsule. Several times, the two crew members had to halt their descent and reach out with hand tools from the open top of the capsule to chip off chunks of rock formations that jutted out and blocked their way.

It took an hour for the men to descend 150 feet. And they became so exhausted, they had to be hoisted back to the 3,700-foot level and replaced by a fresh team.

The next day, the original crew members tried again. This time they were successful in reaching the 4,800-foot level. There they left the capsule and began exploring the dark tunnels. "Hell-o! Hell-o!" they called out as they went.

Flory and Wilkinson were sitting together in the dark when Flory thought he saw light being reflected off the tunnel walls. He blinked, not believing his eyes. Then he heard men's voices and saw miners' headlights.

He and Wilkinson began shouting and beating on the tunnel's water pipes. Within minutes, they were in the arms of their rescuers. The two men had been trapped in the mine for eight days.

Flory and Wilkinson walked slowly with their rescuers to where the capsule waited. Flory was the first to be hauled to the 3,700-foot level. But he refused to be lifted to the surface until Wilkinson could join him and they could leave the mine together.

When it was reported that two men had been found in the mine's lower depths, a great wave of joy swept through the crowd that was waiting within the roped-off area near the mine's entrance. More than a dozen relatives of Flory's and Wilkinson's had joined the throng.

One of Wilkinson's two brothers wept as he waited. The wives of the two men stood in the front row, both of them sobbing.

Flory and Wilkinson were a little wobbly as they walked out of the mine. They had to be supported by fellow miners on each side.

When the two men grinned and waved, the crowd let out a loud cheer. Wilkinson's wife rushed up to embrace him. Flory spotted his wife in the crowd and hurried to her.

Both couples were taken by ambulance to a nearby hospital. When examined, both men were found to be in good condition, although each had lost 14 pounds.

"I'll never go underground again," Wilkinson announced at a hospital press conference.

The discovery of Flory and Wilkinson raised hopes that other miners might still be alive in the maze of tunnels.

But these hopes were soon dashed. As search crews moved toward the bottom of the mine, more and more bodies were discovered. At 5,600 feet, the mine's lowest level, a group of 19 bodies was found.

Those 19 bodies raised the death toll to 91, making the Sunshine Mine disaster one of the worst in

Tom Wilkinson (left) and Ron Flory pose together following their rescue. (Spokane Spokesman Review)

metal-mining history. Larger numbers have been killed in fires and cave-ins, but they have been coal mine accidents.

In the months that followed the fire in the Sunshine Mine, the people of the area tried to put the tragedy behind them. "Life goes on," one man said.

But it was not easy.

"This was the happiest, jolliest town that was ever on the face of the nation," said Mrs. Howard Harrison, whose husband died in the mine of carbon monoxide poisoning. "Do you know what it's like now? It's like a living graveyard."

"It hurts. It hurts," said Mrs. Mike Williams, another woman widowed by the disaster. "I don't know if we'll ever get over it."

· 3 ·

Trapped in the Towers

The nearly 100 small children from the five kindergarten classes at Public School 95 in Brooklyn had just finished admiring the awesome views from the glass-enclosed observation deck on the 107th floor of the South Tower of New York's World Trade Center. The visit was an annual field trip for the school. The date was February 26, 1993.

The teachers and their kindergartners had planned to visit the spacious walkway atop the tower's roof. But it was cold on the roof and a chill wind was blowing. As a result, Trade Center officials had closed the rooftop walkway for the day.

After the children had their lunch in the cafeteria, they got into their coats and jackets and prepared to board the Trade Center's oversize elevators. One hundred seven floors below, buses were waiting that would return them to Brooklyn and their school.

Two of the teachers, Anna Marie Tesoriero and Rosemarie Russo, stood with their classes and watched as the three other classes entered the elevators, and the doors closed. Mrs. Tesoriero's class of 17 kindergartners was next in line. Mrs. Russo and her class, the last to leave the roof, were also the last in line for the elevators.

Just before her children entered an elevator, Mrs. Tesoriero paused to take a snapshot. That done, she guided her class into the elevator for what she thought was to be a 90-second trip to the ground. Other passengers, including several parents of the kindergartners who had gone along on the trip, crowded in before the doors shut.

"We were really squashed," one mother was to say later. "But we thought it was going to be only a few minutes."

As the elevator started downward, Mrs. Tesoriero and the kids began to count off every ten floors — one hundred, ninety, eighty, seventy, and so on.

But at about the halfway point of the descent, everyone felt a hard bump and the elevator jolted to a stop. The lights blinked and went out. The air-conditioning stopped.

What Mrs. Tesoriero, her students, and the others trapped in the elevator didn't know was that a

Rubble in parking garage underneath the World Trade Center. (Wide World)

powerful terrorist bomb had exploded in the under ground garage beneath the twin towers of the World Trade Center. The explosion killed six people, injured many hundreds, and ripped a crater 150 feet wide and several stories deep within the garage.

The tremendous blast not only knocked out the Trade Center's electricity and public address system, it destroyed the backup generators as well. It also demolished the police command center within the huge complex, where plans for emergency operations were kept.

As Mrs. Tesoriero and others in the dark and crowded elevator were beginning to consider their fate, thousands of the Trade Center's approximately 55,000 office workers were seeking to make their way to safety down inky black stairwells through thick smoke.

In the eerie blackness of the stalled elevator, some of the kindergartners started to sob. "I want my mommy," several kids cried.

"We'll be home soon," said Mrs. Tesoriero, "and we'll all see our mommies."

Many of the children sat on the floor clutching adults. "I had one little kid hanging on one leg and another on the other leg," said Ben Reveley, 29, of Cuyama, California. "And I had four hands in one hand."

A few children were becoming panicky. "I'm going to die," one cried out. "That's it. I'm going to die." Teachers and parents sought to comfort the youngsters.

Several of the children eventually fell asleep on the floor. A few went to sleep standing up.

There was no fresh air, and occasionally the trapped passengers would catch a whiff of smoke. This worried Mrs. Tesoriero. Several of her kindergartners suffered from asthma, she knew, and she was concerned that they wouldn't be able to breathe.

It began to get hotter and hotter inside the packed elevator. People took off their winter coats and jackets. Several of the boys removed their shirts.

After more than an hour with no sign of help from the outside, several of the adults pried open the elevator door. The passengers stared out at a blank wall. A little fresh air filtered in. Through the door's opening, someone shouted, "Help! We're in here. Help us!"

The worst part for the passengers was the uncertainty. There was no contact with the outside world, not a word as to what was happening.

Did anyone even know they were trapped?

Two of the kindergarten girls began to sing songs that they had learned for their Thanksgiving pageant. Other children joined in. One of the songs was the theme of Barney, the TV dinosaur: "I love you, you love me, we're a happy family."

After the elevator had been stuck for more than three hours, the lights and air-conditioning suddenly came on. The passengers perked up. When they looked around, they were surprised to see black soot around everyone's mouths. They passed out tissues and cleaned themselves off.

A few minutes later, the lights went off as suddenly as they had gone on and the elevator was plunged into darkness again. Sighs and whimpers could be heard.

Some of the adults began to think that their situation was hopeless, that they were never going to get out of the elevator alive.

Then a voice came over the elevator's speaker. The voice explained it would be a while before the passengers could be rescued because there was another elevator that had to be evacuated first.

This news angered Mrs. Tesoriero. "We have children with asthma here!" she cried out. "We can't wait!"

Everyone stared up at the speaker. But the voice did not respond, and the elevator fell silent again.

Mrs. Tesoriero, her children, and the other passengers were alone with their thoughts and fears again. Meanwhile, Rosemarie Russo and her class of 14 kindergartners were also trapped and facing their own set of problems.

After watching Mrs. Tesoriero and her class board their elevator on the 107th floor, Mrs. Russo then waited for the next elevator. It never arrived.

As she waited, Mrs. Russo noticed the lights blink several times. Then smoke started filtering into the lobby through a door marked EMERGENCY EXIT.

The elevator operator, a man in a red jacket and dark trousers, began speaking excitedly into a portable telephone. Mrs. Russo couldn't hear exactly what he was saying but she caught the words "explosion" and "fire."

More and more smoke filled the air. Suddenly the lights went out. Mrs. Russo knew then that something scary was happening.

Many of the tourists were now milling about. "What's happening?" they kept asking. "What's going on?"

Some of the tourists decided not to wait to find out. They headed for the emergency exit and the stairway leading to the ground level a quarter of a mile below.

Then Mrs. Russo saw the people who operated the gift shop pull down the gates that guarded the shop's windows and lock the doors. The gift shop employees then hurried for the emergency exit.

Mrs. Russo remained calm, even though more black smoke had poured into the observation area. She made up her mind not to go anywhere with her class until she had found out exactly what was happening.

"Don't be frightened," the elevator operator told her. "There may be a smoky fire down below, but it's not going to affect us."

Mrs. Russo found this hard to believe. Shrill alarm bells were going off now. Red emergency lights were flashing.

Then the elevator operator explained to Mrs. Russo that the elevators were no longer operating and that she and her class were going to have to go up to the rooftop walkway, five floors above.

Mrs. Russo gathered the class about her and spoke to them in calm and confident tones. "We can't go home right away," she told them. "Something's happened in the building. Something's wrong. But they're fixing it. As soon as it's fixed, we'll go home." Then she explained that they were going to go up to the walkway on the roof.

Rosemarie Russo guided her class of 14 kindergartners down 107 flights of stairs to safety.
(George Sullivan)

Since the escalator was not running, the class had to ascend the escalator steps one by one. As they made their way up, the air became less smoky, but since there were no lights it kept getting darker and darker. Mrs. Russo instructed the children to interlock their arms and form a chain so that no one would stumble or fall.

Once the class reached the roof, Mrs. Russo found that scores of World Trade Center workers were already there. She also spotted dozens of tourists. The people were walking about the four-sided deck or standing in groups talking. Few were admiring the views.

It was very cold on the roof and a powdery snow was falling, coating the walkway concrete. Mrs. Russo told the children to stay close to a low wall near the escalator exit so they would be shielded from the wind.

Many people came forward to ask Mrs. Russo whether they could help her. "Is there anything I can do for you?" a woman asked. "How can we help?" a couple wanted to know.

A building employee gave Mrs. Russo a coat, and she bundled a child in it. A man offered a pair of gloves and two women gave her warm scarfs for the children.

"One of my little girls was wearing patent leather shoes and anklets," Mrs. Russo said, "and a man who worked in the building picked her up and put her on his shoulders so her feet wouldn't get cold from the snow."

No one on the rooftop seemed to know what had caused the emergency that was unfolding, that a powerful bomb had exploded in the building's parking garage far below.

"We'll be fine," Mrs. Russo told her class. She tried to keep their minds off what was happening by leading them about the promenade, pointing out some of the landmarks — the Statue of Liberty, the Verrazano Narrows Bridge, the Empire State Building, and others.

"Where's our school?" she asked the class. "Can anyone see P.S. Ninety-five?" The children stared out toward Brooklyn through the snow and gloom, but the best they could do was pick out brick buildings that resembled their school.

Mrs. Russo had brought with her a shopping bag filled with supplies in case of an emergency. "You never know with kids," she said. The bag was filled with pretzels and popcorn, raisins and lollipops, which she gave out during the afternoon. Several of the parents who had gone along on the trip had also brought snacks that they shared with the class.

To keep the class amused, Mrs. Russo had the children sing songs that were familiar to them. The class had been preparing a "Salute to Broadway," and so they sang some of the songs that they had been rehearsing, such as "You're a Grand Old Flag" and "Give My Regards to Broadway." Other children and many adults joined in.

"They were fine," Mrs. Russo said of her class. "They forgot about the emergency; they forgot about the cold."

After they had been on the roof for an hour or so, Mrs. Russo was told that the elevators still weren't working and that she and the class might have to be evacuated by helicopter. Police helicopters had been soaring overhead through most of the afternoon.

"We might be going on a helicopter ride," Mrs. Russo told her class. "Isn't that exciting?" Actually, the very idea of a helicopter ride filled Mrs. Russo with alarm. She hoped and prayed it wouldn't be necessary.

Late in the afternoon, with the gray skies growing darker, Mrs. Russo was told that the smoke had cleared in the observation area five floors below, and that they could return there. She then led the class back down the still stalled escalator.

By now, the observation area was hot and stuffy and smelled of smoke. A thin layer of soot coated tables, chairs, and other flat surfaces. From the emergency lights that had been set up, Mrs. Russo could see that the faces of many of the firefighters and rescue workers were blackened with soot.

Then Mrs. Russo was told that since the elevators weren't working, and no one knew when they would be working again, they were going to have to walk down the stairs, all 107 flights. Mrs. Russo shrugged. If it has to be, she thought, it has to be.

Just before the class left the observation area, two of the firefighters performed a thoughtful task. Taking their axes, they broke down the glass door of the gift shop and went inside and snatched up boxes of small souvenir penlights. They then handed out a penlight to each of the kindergartners.

The children were thrilled with their new toys. "They played all kinds of games with them. They used them to play dentist and look in one another's mouths," Mrs. Russo recalled. "They looked in one another's ears."

Led by a firefighter, Mrs. Russo and her class entered the stairwell to begin their long downward trek. The stairwells were pitch-black, but the children used their penlights to brighten the way.

At the 95th floor, the group paused. Emergency workers had set up tables with cookies, milk, and juice for the children. After the class had rested, they returned to the dark stairwell.

The class traveled in single file, with Mrs. Russo leading. On most flights, the children counted out each stair — one, two, three, and so on. "There are twenty stairs in each staircase," said Mrs. Russo with authority.

"Sometimes we'd count backward — twenty, nineteen, eighteen. . . ." said Mrs. Russo. "That's hard for kindergartners to do."

On some of the stairway landings, the group saw stretchers, blankets, and tanks of oxygen, sharp reminders of the emergency in which they were involved.

The children made their way downward without complaining, shining their penlights as they went. "It was an adventure for them," Mrs. Russo said.

At the bottom of each stairwell, Mrs. Russo, who was leading the way, would pause briefly and

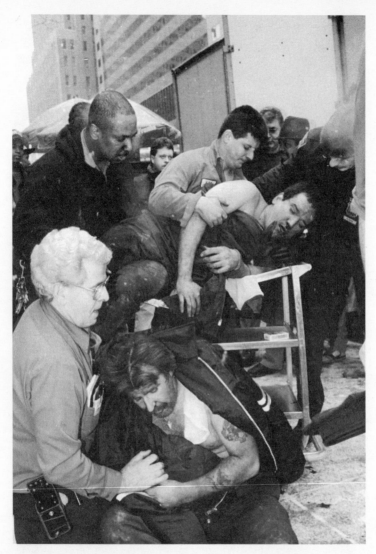

Victims of the explosion that killed six and injured hundreds are helped by rescue personnel. (Wide World)

call out to Dorothy Byrd, her educational assistant, who was the last in line. "Everything okay, Dorothy?" she would say. And Mrs. Russo would also check with the parents who were interspersed throughout the line.

Along the way, the group was often approached by firefighters and rescue workers. "Is everything all right?" they would ask.

Since the floors were numbered, Mrs. Russo and the children always knew how far they had gone, and how far they had to go. "Only seventy-four floors to go," Mrs. Russo would say cheerfully. "We'll get there. We'll get there.

"Just sixty-seven more. Not far. Not far."

The class also sang and whistled as they made their way downward. As they got closer and closer to the ground, the children began to get excited. They shouted out the numbers of the last few floors and started moving faster.

When they finally reached the bottom of the stairs, the children jumped up and down and screamed in delight. "We made it! We made it!" someone shouted. The journey from the roof had taken two and a half hours.

Mrs. Russo and her class of kindergartners were among the very last of those trapped in the World Trade Center to gain their freedom. Mrs. Tesoriero and her class had already been evacuated.

After they had been in the elevator for some four hours, Mrs. Tesoriero and other passengers heard scraping sounds coming from the top of the elevator. It was James Sherwood, a New York City firefighter. From a small office on the 41st floor, Sherwood had broken through the wall of the elevator shaft and climbed onto the elevator's roof.

"How many people in there?" the passengers heard Sherwood shout.

"Seventy-two," someone shouted back.

Sherwood couldn't believe what he had heard. He didn't think the elevator could hold that many people.

"No," he said. "How many *people* do you have in there?"

"Seventy-two," he was told again.

Sherwood opened a hatch in the elevator's roof, then beamed his flashlight down upon the passengers. The kids oohed and aahed. "We're going to get you out now," Sherwood said.

Sherwood passed the flashlight down to one of the passengers. At last the blanket of darkness had been lifted.

Sherwood was surprised that the children seemed calm and that there was no panic, especially when he realized that they had been dangling 41 stories above the ground in a crowded, pitch-black elevator for about four hours.

"You're the bravest kids I've ever seen," he shouted down to the children.

Sherwood was joined by other firefighters. They lowered a ladder through the hatch so the children and others could climb out. After about ten kids, including two of Mrs. Tesoriero's kindergartners, had gone up the ladder into the arms of waiting

Anna Marie Tesoriero leads her kindergarten class to safety after they had been trapped in a World Trade Center elevator for more than four hours. (Wide World)

firefighters, the elevator started to descend in spurts, just a few feet at a time.

The passengers, filled with excitement, clung to one another as the elevator continued to slip downward. When it eased to a stop, everyone cheered.

The doors opened and the passengers piled out. Their ordeal had lasted more than five hours.

Police escorted Mrs. Tesoriero and her class to their bus. The children couldn't understand all the excitement around them. Huge floodlights turned the night into day. There were police officers, firefighters, and rescue workers everywhere. Lights flashed from scores of fire trucks, police cars, and ambulances. Sirens wailed. Was this all for just a bunch of school kids? Then they were told that a bomb had exploded in the garage of the World Trade Center, people had been killed and injured, and everyone was being evacuated from the building.

Mrs. Tesoriero's class had been on the bus for only a short time when they were joined by Mrs. Russo and her class. For the two kindergarten teachers, it was an emotional reunion. They kissed and hugged for several minutes.

Meanwhile, back at Public School 95 in Brooklyn, anxious parents and school officials had been waiting through the afternoon and into the evening for news of Mrs. Tesoriero's class. The other kindergarten classes had all called to report that they were safe. But for several hours, no one knew what had happened to Mrs. Tesoriero's kindergartners. They were simply missing. It wasn't until around six o'clock that Mrs. Tesoriero was able to call the school and report that she and her class had finally been rescued.

Terrorists who planted the bomb were eventually tried and convicted. Here a member of the Terrorist Task Force that was formed gathers evidence from the exit ramp of the Trade Center garage. (Wide World)

Two hours later, when the yellow school bus with Mrs. Russo and Mrs. Tesoriero and their kindergarten classes pulled up outside Public School 95, parents and school officials crowded about the door. One by one, the kids were handed off into the arms of grateful mothers and fathers.

Some of the kids were in tears; others seemed bewildered. Still others were calm.

"I never thought I'd be so happy to see my school," said Mrs. Tesoriero.

Following the bombing at the World Trade Center, the FBI launched one of the biggest investigations of its kind in an effort to bring to justice those responsible for the crime. Their efforts were successful. Four men were arrested and, in 1994, tried and convicted of a long list of charges related to the crime.

Each of the men received a 240-year prison sentence. The sentences made certain that the men would spend the rest of their lives in prison.

In February 1995, police arrested Ramzi Ahmed Yousef in Islamabad, Pakistan, and charged him with being the "mastermind" of the plot. After being returned to the United States, he, too, was convicted and received a long prison sentence.

In the years that followed the bombing, the children from Public School 95 who were involved in the emergency all but forgot their ordeal. Not their parents, however. While they permit their children to go on field trips, the twin towers of the World Trade Center are no longer one of the sites visited. "My son can go to the Bronx Zoo or the Botanical Gardens, to concerts or shows," one mother says, "but nothing with an elevator."

· 4 ·

At the Bottom of the Sea

Early on a crisp, clear May morning in 1939, the sleek, jet-black *Squalus*, the newest of the U.S. Navy's attack submarines, left its pier at the Portsmouth (New Hampshire) Navy Yard and headed out into the Atlantic. Launched several months before, the *Squalus* was under orders to practice a series of high-speed "crash" dives.

Lieutenant Oliver F. Naquin, 35 years old, from Alexandria, Louisiana, a good-looking, stocky man, dark-bearded and soft-spoken, was in command of the vessel, a metal cylinder as long as a football field. The *Squalus* also carried four other officers, three civilian observers, and 51 enlisted men.

While this was a routine mission for the 59 men aboard the *Squalus,* one of a series of tests the vessel was to undergo before being placed on active duty, they were all familiar with the many hazards of serving on a submarine.

To operate beneath the surface of the water, a submarine of the 1930s required air-purifying machinery and a vast array of huge storage batteries and electrical equipment to run the craft when submerged. Crew members constantly faced the danger of being poisoned by chlorine gas generated by the batteries.

In case of an emergency, each crew member had a specific job to perform — to raise or lower the vessel, to start or stop the engines, or to operate pumps. Failure by one crew member to perform an assigned task could mean death to all.

Several miles out of Portsmouth, the *Squalus* glided past the cluster of reefs that make up the Isles of Shoals. A few miles beyond, the *Squalus* prepared to dive, an operation that involved flooding the ballast tanks with water. With the added weight, the *Squalus* would lose its ability to stay afloat and slip below the surface.

Machinist's mate Alfred Prien stood before the control board, called the "Christmas tree" because of its many red and green lights. His orders were to take the *Squalus* to a depth of 50 feet as quickly as possible.

The diving signal flashed. The engines stopped. A siren blared.

Prien spun the controls. A series of green lights glittered, showing Prien that the air induction valves, which sucked air into the engine and engine room, were closed and watertight.

The *Squalus* dipped below the surface. Prien pushed the control wheel forward, adjusting the diving planes to make the submarine descend. He watched the depth gauge: . . . 20 feet . . . 30 feet . . . 40 feet . . . 50 feet. Prien pulled back on the control wheel to level off.

Suddenly, Prien heard a frantic message from the engine room: "Water coming in!"

Prien rechecked the lights on the control panel. All were green, indicating all valves were shut.

But they were not. One of the induction valves was still open and it was now sucking not air but water into the compartments that housed the engine room.

"Blow the ballast and ascend!" Prien heard Lieutenant Naquin order. Prien pulled hard on the control wheel and the ship's bow bolted upward at close to a 45-degree angle. Prien grabbed at the control panel in an effort to stay on his feet.

As Prien struggled in front of the controls, the submarine's lights went out. Slowly, quietly, the *Squalus* began to slide stern-first toward the bottom.

Electrician's mate Lloyd Maness was at the bulkhead door between the *Squalus's* control room and engine room. His buddies called Maness a "swell little guy." In an emergency, it was Maness's job to close the door, then "dog it down," or seal it.

Maness tugged at the heavy metal door, which because of the submarine's angle had to be swung in an upward direction. He had almost gotten it closed when he heard shouts from the engine room: "Keep it open! Keep it open!"

Maness let the door fall back and five men struggled through to safety. Water surged after them. Maness put his shoulder to the door and swung it shut again, then turned down the clamps, making it watertight.

As Maness walked forward to join the rest of the crew, he fully realized that there were men still trapped in the flooded compartments. One of them was Sherman Shirley, a good friend. Shirley had been planning to be married the next Sunday, and Maness was to be his best man at the wedding.

But Maness had no regrets about closing the door. If he had not done so, the entire submarine would have flooded. With his heroic act he had saved not only his own life but the lives of 32 others.

The *Squalus* drifted downward to settle on the bottom, 240 feet below the surface. There the vessel lay helplessly, a long steel cylinder, without heat, without power to operate its radio equipment, and without the means of pumping out the water that had flooded the engine room and other sections of its hull.

In the silence and darkness of the submarine's dry compartments, the trapped men began to

Rescue operations for the sunken Squalus *were conducted from the U.S.S.* Falcon *(right). The rescue chamber can be seen on the* Falcon's *after deck.*
(*Naval Historical Foundation*)

wait. They were familiar with the navy's poor record of coping with submarine disasters. Between 1919 and 1927, eight submarines had gone to the bottom. In only a few cases had any crew members been saved.

There was no panic aboard the *Squalus*. There were plenty of grim faces, however, as the tense crew members prepared to face a situation each had lived in dread of from the first moments he had entered submarine service. It was as if everyone's worst nightmare were coming true.

Small battery-powered lamps were lighted and hung in the main compartments. No one would go hungry, for there was plenty of canned food.

With no heat and no power, the temperature dropped quickly. There was enough oxygen for about 48 hours.

Lieutenant Naquin was calm. He issued orders in a confident voice to his dungaree-clad crew, and they hurried to carry them out. The lieutenant had faith that navy rescuers would save them.

The men wrapped themselves in blankets from the officers' quarters. Lieutenant Naquin told them to lie down to conserve oxygen and their energy.

The men spoke quietly with one another, discussing the various methods the navy might use in rescuing them.

When Lieutenant Naquin overheard someone mention the men who were trapped in the flooded engine room, he told the man to "knock it off." Nothing could be done then for those men, the lieutenant explained. Talking about them could only serve to dampen the spirits of the survivors.

From the forward compartment of the *Squalus*, Lieutenant Naquin fired smoke bombs, which were to ignite on the surface and mark where the vessel had gone down. He also released a cylinder-shaped marker buoy, a bright yellow can about as long as a baseball bat, that contained a telephone. A wire connected the telephone to a second telephone aboard the *Squalus*.

All of the crewmen aboard the *Squalus* were trained in the use of the Momsen lung, a breathing device sometimes relied upon in undersea emergencies. A storage compartment in the control room of the *Squalus* contained a supply of Momsen lungs, and Lieutenant Naquin ordered that one be given to each man.

But no one looked forward to using the device. It represented a gamble.

The Momsen lung looked like a gas mask. It fitted over the face and clamped shut over the wearer's nose as he gripped a mouthpiece between his teeth, then inhaled oxygen through the mouthpiece from a small tank strapped to the chest.

Once the men had put on their Momsen lungs, a circular escape hatch in the submarine's deck would be opened and a line floated to the surface. One by one, the men would ascend the line to freedom.

The danger in using this method of escape had to do with the depth at which the *Squalus* rested — 240 feet. Ascending too rapidly from such a depth, from an atmosphere of water at high pressure into air at ordinary pressure, could cause bubbles of nitrogen to form in the bloodstream, a condition known as the bends. Severe pain, even paralysis, could be the result.

No one wanted to risk that. Lieutenant Naquin assured the men that the Momsen lungs would be used only as a last resort.

Meanwhile, back at the Portsmouth Navy Yard, concern was building for the *Squalus*. About an hour after the submarine's departure, a radiogram had been received from the *Squalus* that announced: "Preparing to dive for one hour."

Later, when the yard attempted to contact the *Squalus*, there was no answer. Within minutes, the *Sculpin*, a sister ship to the *Squalus*, was sent to look for the silent sub. (At the time, the navy named its submarines after fish. The sculpin is a freshwater fish commonly called the bullhead; the squalus is a small shark known as the dogfish.)

It didn't take lookouts aboard the *Sculpin* long to spot a red smudge on the ocean surface created by one of the smoke bombs that Lieutenant Naquin had released. And moments later they found the telephone buoy.

In the cold and clammy compartments of the *Squalus*, smiles lit the faces of the crewmen when they heard the steady thump of the *Sculpin*'s engines. They knew they had been found. It had been about four hours since the *Squalus* had left its Portsmouth pier.

Lieutenant Naquin spoke by telephone to the commanding officer of the *Sculpin*. He explained that an induction valve was open when his submarine dived, that the after compartments had flooded as a result, and that the vessel was now resting on the bottom at a depth of 240 feet.

Lieutenant Naquin said that he did not want to try escaping with Momsen lungs. It was too risky. He suggested instead that a diver be sent down to close the open valve and attach salvage hoses to the flooded compartments to pump the water out. Then the submarine would float to the surface.

Suddenly, the waves jerked the *Sculpin* to one side, and the telephone line snapped. The *Squalus* was cut off from its rescuers. The captain of the *Sculpin* anchored over its sister ship and waited for instructions.

Some of the trapped men in the forward compartment of the *Squalus* found hammers and began to tap out Morse code messages on the vessel's steel hull. That evening, the *Sculpin* picked up one of the messages. It said: "Conditions satisfactory, but cold."

As soon as the disaster that struck the *Squalus* became known, newspaper reporters and photographers flocked to the Portsmouth Navy Yard, which served as headquarters for the rescue operations. Hotels were soon filled for miles around, and many newsmen spent the night sleeping on chairs or sofas in hotel lobbies.

The navy provided an oceangoing tugboat for reporters. It made several trips to and from Portsmouth and the rescue scene. At the height of rescue operations, more than 300 newspaper and radio reporters were on hand.

By daybreak on the first morning after the *Squalus* had gone down, a small fleet hovered in the blue water above the sunken craft. Besides the *Sculpin*, the vessels included the rescue ship *Falcon*, Coast Guard cutters, a navy tug, and several small fishing boats carrying newspaper reporters and photographers.

That afternoon, the cruiser *Brooklyn*, carrying about 50 newspaper reporters, arrived from the Brooklyn Navy Yard. The yellow telephone buoy floated at the center of the clustered boats.

The best hope of the men trapped aboard the *Squalus* rested on the deck of the *Falcon* in the form of a huge steel rescue chamber. The nine-ton, bell-shaped chamber, ten feet high, eight feet in diameter at the top, had been developed by Commander Allan McCann. He, along with other navy rescue experts, was directing operations from aboard the *Falcon*.

Twelve years before, Commander McCann had been a young officer aboard a navy ship in the water above the navy submarine *S-4* after it had sunk in the Atlantic off Provincetown, Massachusetts. Forty men had died in the disaster.

McCann was shocked that the navy had no practical method of rescuing the men trapped aboard the *S-4*. In the years that followed the *S-4* tragedy, McCann worked to develop the bell-shaped chamber that had been placed on the deck of the *Falcon*. Sometimes it was referred to as the McCann diving bell.

Inside the bell-shaped rescue chamber: Squalus *crew members climbed out of the submarine, then through the circular hatch into the rescue chamber's upper compartment.* (Wide World)

About 24 hours after the *Squalus* had gone down, a diver was lowered from the *Falcon* to the submarine, 240 feet below. He slid a shackle through a ring in the submarine's deck and attached a steel cable to the shackle.

When the men imprisoned on the *Squalus* heard the diver at work, they breathed a collective sigh of relief. They knew that rescue operations had begun.

Meanwhile, the diving chamber had been lowered into the water over the side of the *Falcon*. Using the cable put in place by the diver, the chamber with its two-man crew began pulling itself down toward the *Squalus*.

The chamber was made up of two separate compartments, one atop the other, divided by a watertight hatch. The two crew members occupied the upper compartment. The lower compartment had an open bottom.

Once the chamber's lower compartment was in place over a hatch on the deck of the *Squalus*, the water in that compartment was blown out. The pressure from water outside then worked to clamp the chamber to the hull of the *Squalus* like a suction cup.

The crewmen aboard the chamber opened the hatch between the upper and lower compartments. They then entered the lower compartment. The next step was to open the hatch on the submarine's deck.

When the submarine's hatch fell open, a wave of joy swept over the trapped men. Some cheered, some clapped.

Seven members of the *Squalus*'s crew got ready to climb into the rescue chamber. Lieutenant Naquin had designated one officer (to report on conditions below), one civilian, and the five individuals in the worst condition to go in the first group. The men who were to remain aboard the *Squalus* accepted the lieutenant's decision in customary silence.

Wrapped in blankets, a group of rescued crew members arrives by Coast Guard boat at the Portsmouth Navy Yard. (Wide World)

Once the submarine's hatch had been sealed shut and the seven men were safe in the upper compartment of the rescue chamber, the hatch between the two compartments was closed. The rescue chamber then made its way to the surface.

Two of the rescued men were laughing as they stepped out of the chamber onto the deck of the *Falcon*. Another man stumbled and several sailors reached out to grab him.

The first men ever rescued by the McCann chamber, the group of seven was whisked by a Coast Guard boat to the Naval Yard hospital in Portsmouth.

Later that afternoon, nine more men were brought to the deck of the *Falcon*. Three hours later, another group of nine men reached safety. On the rescue chamber's third trip to the *Squalus*, blankets and containers of milk and hot soup were sent down to Lieutenant Naquin and the other seven men who remained below.

When news of the sinking of the *Squalus* became known, the families and relatives of the men trapped aboard the vessel were filled with great anxiety. The crew members were fathers, husbands, and brothers. Who had survived? Who had not? At first, no one knew.

Families waited at home by their radios for the latest news. (There was no television in those days.) When rescue operations began, wives and other relatives who lived in and near Portsmouth went to the Navy Yard and gathered at the Administration Building.

The wife of Carlton Powell, a machinist's mate second class from Cardiff-by-the-Sea, California, waited for hours in a hallway of the Administration Building for news of her husband. Finally, when her husband's name was read with the names of others who were described as being "alive and well," she was quiet for a moment and then began laughing hysterically.

The wife of Lawrence Gainor, a chief electrician's mate from Honolulu, Hawaii, received the news of her husband's survival more calmly, with a sense of relief.

When Mrs. Gainor inquired about the husband of a close friend, she was told his name was not on the list. Mrs. Gainor hung her head. In releasing the names of the survivors, the navy had announced, "Names omitted from this list are probably in flooded compartments, and there is little hope of finding them alive."

On the fourth and final trip to the *Squalus*, the rescue chamber brought up eight men, including Lieutenant Naquin, the last man to leave the submarine. On this last dive, one of the chamber's cables snagged and had to be cut. There were some tense moments before the chamber finally rested safely on the deck of the *Falcon*.

The navy then issued a final bulletin, saying, "This completes the rescue of all known survivors."

Another act in the tragic drama of the *Squalus* was played out the next day. Many of the relatives and friends of the 26 men trapped in the flooded engine room of the *Squalus* clung to the hope that some of them might still be alive, even though the navy had classified the men as "unaccounted for and presumed dead."

To satisfy the doubts, the navy agreed to continue its rescue efforts. The next day, the rescue chamber was lowered again, this time to an escape hatch leading to the *Squalus*'s engine room.

The crew worked carefully. After the rescue chamber was secured to the deck of the submarine, the two crewmen lowered themselves to the escape hatch. Slowly they opened it. They knew if there happened to be air inside there was hope that some of the men might still be alive. If they saw water, there could be no hope.

When the men peered into the black interior of the submarine, they saw nothing but water. It filled the hatch to the very top, spilling over the raised metal rim into which the hatch cover fitted.

The men reported the tragic news to the *Falcon*. Sadly, they closed the hatch and dogged it shut. Then the diving chamber was raised to the surface. The navy's rescue mission of the submarine *Squalus* had ended.

There is a strange and tragic footnote to the story of the *Squalus*. The vessel was later raised, repaired, and sent to sea again with a new name, the *Sailfish*. When the United States entered World War II in 1941, the *Sailfish* went on active duty in the Pacific.

So did the *Sculpin*, the submarine that had played a vital role in the rescue of the *Squalus*. In November 1943, however, the *Sculpin's* tour of duty came to a luckless end. Sighted by a Japanese destroyer, the *Sculpin* was forced to the surface by depth charges and was then sunk by the destroyer's guns.

But dozens of the *Sculpin's* crew members managed to escape from the stricken vessel before it went down. The Japanese picked up 42 survivors. Twenty of these men were put aboard the Japanese aircraft carrier *Chuyo,* presumably to be transported to Japan to be interned as prisoners of war.

The *Chuyo* never reached its destination. Early in December 1943, on the voyage to Japan, the

Squalus *was later raised, repaired, and returned to service as the U.S.S.* Sailfish. *Here the vessel is pictured at dock at the Portsmouth (New Hampshire) Navy Yard before repair work began.* (Wide World)

Chuyo was torpedoed and sunk by an American submarine. The submarine that dealt the death blow to the *Chuyo*, its Japanese crew, and 20 American submariners from the *Sculpin* was the *Sailfish*.

• 5 •

Trapped on Everest

When Jon Krakauer, a veteran mountain climber and journalist, reached the summit of Mount Everest early on the afternoon of May 10, 1996, he didn't feel like celebrating. He was colder than he had ever been in his life and he was so tired he could hardly lift his feet. All he really wanted to do was get back down the mountain.

Krakauer collected a few small stones as souvenirs, then snapped a few quick photographs of Andy Harris, a guide with the expedition of which he was a member, and Anatoli Boukreev, a Russian guide with another expedition. Krakauer spent only about five minutes at the highest spot on planet Earth.

Just before leaving the summit, Krakauer happened to look down and spotted a blanket of clouds drifting up from the valleys below. Already they obscured some of the smaller peaks below Everest.

Krakauer was filled with anxiety. But his nervous state had little to do with the clouds. When he checked, he found that his last oxygen tank was almost empty. He needed to get to a lower altitude fast. His life depended on it.

Those swirling clouds that Jon Krakauer saw that afternoon were more significant than he realized. They signaled the arrival of a brutal storm that would strike with full fury later in the day. It turned what had been a good climbing afternoon into a nightmare. Temperatures dropped to below zero and kept plunging until windchill figures were in triple digits. Snow whipped by ferocious winds blinded climbers.

Over the next 36 hours, the slopes of Mount Everest would become a vast, trackless death trap. Eight people would die, including Rob Hall, who headed Krakauer's climbing team. Some of those who survived had fingers and toes so frostbitten that they had to be amputated.

Several months later, in an interview with Tom Brokaw on *Internight*, Krakauer declared, "I wish I never heard of Everest."

Mount Everest, one of the Himalayas, the mountain range that extends for about 1,500 miles along the border between Nepal and Tibet, is, simply, the highest mountain in the world.

Jon Krakauer, of Seattle, Washington, a journalist and veteran climber, was one of the surviving members of the 1996 Everest expeditions. (Wide World)

How high is it? The answer is debated. Most mountaineering groups accept 29,002 feet (about 5½ miles), the figure arrived at by the British government in the 1850s.

In 1954, the Surveyor General of the Republic of India set the height at 29,028 feet, plus or minus 10 feet depending on snow conditions. The National Geographic Society accepts this figure.

In 1987, a new figure based on satellite measurements put Mount Everest's height at 29,864 feet, but that figure has not been widely accepted.

No matter which figure is used, Mount Everest towers high above all North American mountains. Alaska's Mount McKinley, at 20,320 feet the highest mountain on the North American continent, is merely shoulder high to Mount Everest. And California's Mount Whitney, at 14,494 feet the tallest peak in the Lower 48, is only about one half of Everest's size.

The highest mountain in the world was first identified as such by Sir George Everest in 1849. From that day, humans have tried to climb it. Sir Edmund Hillary, a New Zealander, and Tenzing Norgay, a Nepalese Sherpa climber, became the first to reach Everest's summit, in 1953. The first American to reach the top did so in 1963, the first woman in 1975.

In the years since Everest was first conquered, more than 4,000 climbers have tried to reach the top. Of these, about 650 have succeeded. In 1993, 40 climbers reached Everest's summit on a single day.

But climbers have paid a heavy price. About 150 have died in attempting to reach Everest's summit.

One problem is that not all of those who challenge the mountain are skilled and experienced mountaineers. Thanks to improvements in equipment and clothing, which have made Everest easier to climb, more and more amateurs make the attempt every year, and not all are qualified to make it. Some are attracted by advertisements in climbing magazines that offer places in "commercial Everest expeditions."

For a "tourist climber," the cost can be as much as $65,000. And there's no refund if the expedition leader decides the group can't make it and turns back.

On that luckless May weekend in 1996, about 150 climbers had assembled at various camps on Everest's lower stretches, all eager to set foot on the top.

Some 30 belonged to two separate expeditions under the supervision of Scott Fischer from Seattle and New Zealander Rob Hall. As professional guides, Fischer and Hall were considered among the best in the world.

Fischer, 40 years old, headed the Mountain Madness expedition. Charming and easygoing, a strong climber, Fischer had been to Everest several times before and had reached the summit in 1994. But this was the first trip in which he acted as a commercial guide.

Fischer's expedition offered two guides besides himself — Neal Beidleman, a seasoned high-altitude climber from Aspen, Colorado, and Anatoli Boukreev, a noted Russian mountaineer.

Fischer's clients included Sandy Hill Pittman, a former New York fashion editor with a fair amount of climbing experience; Charlotte Fox and her boyfriend, Tim Madsen, a pair of ski patrol members from Aspen, Colorado; Lene Gammelgaard, from Copenhagen, Denmark, who was seeking to become the first Scandinavian woman to conquer Everest; and two others.

Most observers agreed that Fischer's group included several people who were not particularly well qualified as climbers. Rob Hall's expedition was looked upon as the stronger of the two.

Hall, 35 years old, the founder of Adventure Consultants, had been on the summit four times and had guided 17 clients there, more than any other professional guide.

In contrast to the relaxed style of Scott Fischer, who, as one climber put it, "cut his clients a lot of slack," Hall was stricter and paid careful attention to detail. Every day was carefully planned. Every step was taken under the close watch of a guide or Hall himself. Hall kept a careful count of the team's oxygen cannisters and even checked the sharpness of his clients' crampons, the toothed metal spikes that prevent slipping when walking on ice or hard-packed snow.

Hall's group included two guides, Mike Groom, an Australian with long experience as a climber, and Andy Harris, also from Australia. The likable

Lene Gammelgaard, of Copenhagen, Denmark, became the first Scandinavian woman to climb the world's highest mountain. (Wide World)

Harris was a junior guide who had never climbed above 23,000 feet.

Jon Krakauer, mentioned earlier, also a member of the Hall expedition, was a mountaineer as well as an author. Krakauer planned to transmit day-by-day accounts of the climb on a Web site. And he would later write a full account of the weekend for *Outside*, an outdoors magazine published in Santa Fe, New Mexico. Still later, Krakauer wrote a best-selling book, *Into Thin Air*, about the disastrous climb.

Hall's clients also included Beck Weathers, a wealthy pathologist from Texas. Weathers was about to celebrate his fiftieth birthday. His Everest adventure was a birthday gift to himself.

Yasuko Namba, a 47-year-old Japanese climber, was the only female member of Hall's group. She had high hopes of becoming the oldest woman ever to make the Everest climb.

Doug Hansen, another member of Hall's group, was a postal worker from Renton, Washington. Hansen's climb was being paid for, at least in part, by elementary school children from Kent, Washington, who had sold T-shirts on Hansen's behalf. Although Hansen had climbed Everest before, and come close to reaching the summit, he was perhaps the slowest climber in Hall's group.

A Canadian doctor, an Australian doctor, a lawyer from Michigan, and a publisher from Hong Kong were also part of the Hall expedition.

Both groups were aided by several Sherpas, a Tibetan people living on the high southern slopes of the Himalayas in eastern Nepal. These assistants were the backbone of every climb. They established the campsites and erected the tents, made tea, did the cooking, set the climbing ropes, and carried the heaviest loads. Tourist climbers seldom carried more than daypacks, which contained their personal belongings, and, when necessary, their own oxygen tanks.

Some Sherpas claimed that a big, hairy, manlike creature they called *yeti,* or the Abominable Snowman, lived amid the snows and mists at Everest's summit. On this expedition, there would be no talk of *yeti.* There would be too much else to worry about.

You don't climb Mount Everest over a weekend. The venture takes months of planning and is done in stages.

Serious climbing begins at Base Camp, a collection of green, blue, and yellow dome-shaped tents pitched at 17,600 feet. Some climbers spend as long as a month at Base Camp getting used to the altitude.

In the spring of 1996, Jon Krakauer recalled, Base Camp was crowded with climbers. It was "like Times Square." It sheltered people of all nationalities, both sexes, and every level of climbing skill and experience. The mess tent offered excellent food. There were fax machines and hot showers. Starbucks Coffee had an outpost at Base Camp that year.

Operating from Base Camp, climbers establish several other camps, each at a higher level than the previous one. They spend several days at each one.

At Camp 1, at 20,000 feet, almost four miles in the sky, tents are set out on narrow sections of ice that make up the perilous Khumbu Ice Fall. On either side are crevasses so deep that they seem bottomless.

Camp 2, at 21,000 feet, is built on a long stretch of glacier ice. Kept stocked with food and fuel, it is also known as the Advance Base Camp. Camp 3 is another 2,250 feet higher.

When a team is ready, climbers ascend to Camp 4. At 26,000 feet, Camp 4 is laid out on what is called South Col, a flat and desolate shale-strewn patch the size of several football fields in between the peaks of Everest and Lhotse, which is the fourth-highest mountain in the world.

During the 1996 climbing season, Camp 4 was littered with shredded scraps of tent fabric, dozens of yellow, red, and green oxygen tanks, used-up batteries, and an occasional empty box of raisins and M&M's wrappers. There were also a couple of human skeletons there, still zipped into their down parkas, which gave an eerie feeling to the place.

It takes about 12 hours to cover the mile-and-a-half route from Camp 4 to the summit. This stretch is known as the Death Zone — and for good reason.

At 20,000 feet and beyond, the altitude and extreme cold present very serious hazards. The air has only one third the oxygen found in air at sea level. While climbers carry tanks of oxygen, they constantly run the risk of suffering oxygen deprivation and becoming confused and light-headed. "Your brain shuts down," said Jon Krakauer. "You feel like a six-year-old." Headaches, hacking coughs, and vomiting are also common.

The bitter cold can lead to hypothermia, a condition of abnormally low body temperature. You want to go to sleep. But close your eyes and you can pass out and die.

Under such conditions, climbers can trek no more than half a mile a day. Your legs may be able to travel more, but you're slowed by the struggle to cope with the cold, the altitude, and the lack of oxygen.

By the afternoon of May 9, 1996, the Fischer and Hall expeditions had pitched their tents at Camp 4 and had started making preparations for the final push to the summit.

The climb to reach Camp 4 had been a difficult one for Scott Fischer. He had been up and down the mountain assisting climbers, one of whom had become ill and had to be taken back to Base Camp. And one of Fischer's Sherpas was stricken with a severe case of altitude sickness. Fischer supervised the man's evacuation by helicopter to a

Scott Fischer, leader of the Mountain Madness expedition, had been to Everest's summit several times before his luckless climb in 1996. (Wide World)

hospital in Kathmandu, the capital of Nepal. That night Fischer slept soundly.

Other climbers in the Fischer expedition also rested, waiting for a storm to pass. Some sipped tea or hot chocolate. Loss of appetite is common at high altitudes, but those who felt like eating munched candy bars.

Late in the evening, after the weather had cleared, the climbers got ready to move out. Each got into a harness, the assortment of belts and straps used to fasten the climber to the guide ropes, and strapped on their crampons.

Each climber also clamped on a rubber oxygen mask and hooked up to a fresh tank of oxygen. A cannister of oxygen, which weighed about seven pounds, would last from five and a half to six hours. Each climber carried a second tank, and a third was to be supplied by the Sherpas.

Three bottles added up to almost 18 hours of oxygen. That figured to be enough to get a climber to the summit, allow for a pause of a few minutes, and still give each enough time to get back down to Camp 4.

Since it was pitch-black when the climbers set out from Camp 4, they lighted their way with headlamps. But not long after they departed, a brilliant moon ascended in the sky, and the climbers were able to douse the lights.

Rob Hall was confident, believing the effort was going to be a smash success. So was Scott Fischer. "We're going to pop this thing," he said.

Hall's group led the way. Through the early morning hours, all went well, even though it was slow going. The first in a series of troublesome delays occurred when the first climbers reached the Southeast Ridge, one of the most exposed parts of the ascent.

Hall and Fischer had agreed before leaving Base Camp that a party of Sherpas would leave the camp well before the rest of the climbers to break trail and put in the fixed ropes along the upper stretches of the mountain leading to the summit. Such ropes are vital. They make the ascent safer and faster, especially for inexperienced climbers.

But the Sherpas had not installed the ropes. When the first climbers reached several huge rock obstacles at 28,000 feet, they were stopped dead in their tracks. They waited at the base of the obstacle, all the while sucking precious oxygen.

Eventually, Neal Beidleman, one of the guides from Fischer's group, offered to install the ropes himself. Once the ropes were in place, the climbers were able to make their way to the South Summit, some 330 vertical feet below the top, which was now in everyone's clear view.

There was some concern about Scott Fischer, who had not been seen by anyone. He had announced earlier that he would be trailing his group. In that way, he said, he would be able to help any stragglers. But even with the delay, Fischer had not caught up.

The toughest part of the climb was just ahead, a rock face about 40 feet high that led to a narrow crevasse called the Hillary Step. But again no guide ropes were in place. And again the climbers sat and waited, stacking up like supermarket shoppers in a checkout line.

This time, Fischer's two guides, Beidleman and Boukreev, plus one of Rob Hall's guides, Andy Harris, moved out ahead to string the ropes. Jon Krakauer also helped. But another hour had been wasted.

With ropes in place, the climbers plodded toward the top, one heavy step at a time, taking in two or three gulps of oxygen with each step.

Boukreev was the first to reach the summit, followed by two other guides, Harris and Beidleman, and then Krakauer. About 20 minutes later, other climbers from Fischer's group began to arrive.

Everest's summit is a slender shelf of rock and ice that covers about the same area as a small room. A climber in Hall's group recalled seeing a discarded oxygen cannister, an aluminum survey pole, and a string of wind-whipped Buddhist prayer flags at the top.

The sky was a brilliant blue. The awesome views included the other towering Himalayan peaks, some almost as high as Everest itself, and the vast panorama across the Tibetan plateau into Tibet and Nepal. Sandy Hill Pittman, looking down from the top, said that she could "actually see the curve of the earth."

Jon Krakauer felt little excitement upon reaching the top, even though he had achieved a lifelong goal. He was troubled by the realization that the summit marked the halfway point of the expedition. The long, hazardous descent lay ahead, and he was running short on oxygen.

Something else bothered Krakauer. When he looked down, he could see clouds rising out of the valley below. He guessed they were the tops of storm clouds, and he was right.

Krakauer wasted no time at the top. As others were arriving, he turned and started back down. He passed Rob Hall, the leader of his group, who was pushing his way up. Krakauer thanked Hall for helping him to get to the top. "Yeah, it turned out to be a pretty good expedition," Hall said.

Back at the summit, Beidleman looked at his watch. It was shortly after 3:00 P.M. Where was Fischer? Beidleman decided that he and the climbers with him could wait no longer for him. "Scott's not here," Beidleman announced, "but we gotta get the hell outta here." The climbers were now using their last bottles of oxygen. Any more delays could be tragic.

On the way down, Beidleman and the others passed Fischer, who was plodding his way toward the summit. With Fischer was Ming Ho Gau, an experienced Taiwanese climber. Beidleman and Fischer waved and spoke a few words. Beidleman figured that Fischer would turn around immediately after reaching the top. He fully expected him to be right behind him before too long.

Krakauer and Boukreev also passed Fischer as he struggled toward the summit. To Krakauer, Fischer looked "hammered." Fischer also looked fatigued to Boukreev, but he saw no cause for alarm. Boukreev knew Fischer to be very strong.

When Fischer finally did reach the summit, he radioed Base Camp: "Everybody made it, but I'm so tired."

As Fischer paused at the top, his clients and Hall's were continuing down the mountain. Harris and Krakauer led the way, followed by Beidleman and the group he was leading.

As the climbers descended, the weather began to turn ugly. Thick clouds boiled up from below to envelop them. The temperature nose-dived, a stiff wind began to blow, and it started snowing.

By late afternoon, with the visibility at zero, the weary climbers found themselves in the midst of a deadly whiteout. Wind-whipped snow, blowing sideways, stabbed at the climbers' faces. As the temperature kept dropping, any exposed skin was instantly frozen. The women and men on Everest's slopes were trapped in a fierce struggle for their lives.

An exhausted Jon Krakauer managed to make it to Camp 4 and the safety of his tent. So did Fischer's guide, Anatoli Boukreev.

The others were not so fortunate. Blowing like a hurricane, the deadly storm overtook Neal Beidleman and the climbers in his group, and they struggled to reach Camp 4. It caught Scott Fischer

Doug Hansen, from Renton, Washington, ran out of oxygen on Everest, collapsed, and died. (Wide World)

and Ming Ho Gau a thousand feet below the summit. And it trapped Rob Hall and Doug Hansen, the postal worker from Renton, Washington, whom Hall had stopped to help, just below the top.

Beidleman and his party had staggered through the snow and cold along the narrow Southeast Ridge, within sight of the tents of Camp 4, no more than a mile and a half away. Then darkness fell, cutting visibility to a few yards. Beidleman and the others became lost, without any idea of how to find the tents.

The group stumbled about in the storm. On either side were sheer drops of 4,000 feet. Afraid that someone would fall off the face of the mountain, Beidleman, yelling at the top of his lungs, got everyone to huddle together to wait out the storm.

Not long after midnight, the clouds lifted, and Beidleman and some of the others could make out the stars and constellations. Using the stars as reference points, members of the group were able to figure out where the tents should be.

Beidleman began screaming at his climbers over the roaring wind, telling them to get to their feet. But several would not. So Beidleman, together with guide Mike Groom, stumbled back to Camp 4, leading those who would walk.

At the tents, Boukreev was waiting. Before the exhausted Beidleman collapsed in his tent, he told Boukreev there were others still out on the mountain and how to find them.

Grabbing extra tanks of oxygen, Boukreev headed out into the night. Finding no one, he returned to the camp to get better instructions from Beidleman. Then he set out again.

When Boukreev came upon Sandy Hill Pittman, Charlotte Fox, and Tim Madsen, he found them to be almost unconscious. He gave Pittman and Madsen a bottle of oxygen to share. Fox seemed to be in better shape than anyone else, but she still could not walk. Boukreev lugged her back to camp.

When Boukreev returned, he put Pittman on his back and hauled her to the tents. Madsen trudged along behind.

On his third trip into the night, Boukreev found Yasuko Namba's body. She had frozen to death.

The next morning, more rescuers set out to bring back those still trapped. A team of Sherpas found Scott Fischer and Ming Ho Gau, both barely alive. Fischer could not move. The Sherpas left Fischer with oxygen and headed back with Gau, whom they thought might live.

Later in the day, Boukreev went back up the mountain and found Fischer dead. Apparently delirious at the end, he had removed his gloves and unzipped his jacket. Boukreev dragged Fischer's body off the path, lashed it to the mountain, and covered his face. Then Boukreev headed back in the dark.

The next day, Gau was helicoptered off of Everest by Lieutenant Colonel Madan Khatri Chetri, a

After a close brush with death, Beck Weathers, of Dallas, Texas, suffering from severe frostbite on his face and hands, was plucked by rescue helicopter from Everest's slopes. (Wide World)

Nepalese pilot. Helicopters rarely fly above 20,000 feet because the air is so thin it reduces their lift. The daring Madan managed to hover just above the snow's surface at Camp 2 as Gau was put aboard.

After delivering Gau to Base Camp, Madan returned to the upper reaches of the mountain to rescue Beck Weathers, who had staged a miraculous recovery. Rescuers had left Weathers behind, thinking he was lifeless. But later Weathers, after lying unconscious for three or four hours, came staggering into Camp 4, his right ungloved hand, horribly frostbitten, stretched out in front of him.

A month later, back in the United States, surgeons had to amputate Weathers's hand. Gau lost fingers and toes to frostbite.

Everest had already taken a heavy toll. Scott Fischer and Yasuko Namba were dead. Ming Ho Gau and Beck Weathers had narrowly escaped death, but both suffered serious injuries.

There were to be other victims that weekend. Far up the mountain, Rob Hall lay trapped. After reaching the summit, Hall had waited more than an hour for the 46-year-old Doug Hansen to arrive. Then he and Hansen headed down together. On the way down, Hansen ran out of oxygen and collapsed.

Hall stayed through the night in a snow hole at the South Summit with Hansen. The next morning, he could not move. Hansen died during the night.

Two Sherpas set out from Camp 4 to rescue Hall. They fought their way up the mountain. But the weather kept getting worse, and with only about 200 yards to go they were forced to turn back.

Hall kept in radio communication with Base Camp throughout the day. His friends there urged him to make the descent under his own power.

Hall replied that there was something wrong with his legs and he was not able to walk. Hall's friends thought it was a miracle that he was still alive, considering that he had spent the night without shelter, fluids, or food while being blasted by hurricane-force winds at something below minus-100-degree windchill.

Later in the day, Hall managed to make a satellite telephone call to his wife in New Zealand. In a voice that was weak from exposure, Hall did his best not to alarm her. "Please don't worry too much," he said.

These may have been his last words. Twelve days later, a pair of climbers on their way to the summit found Hall's body partly buried in a snowdrift.

The young guide Andy Harris was also dead. At about the same time that Hall's body was found, climbers from another expedition discovered Harris's ice ax planted on a exposed ridge near the South Summit. No one knows for certain how Harris died. His body was never found.

There were other victims that weekend. On the other side of Everest, that is, on the northern approach to the top, three members of the Indo-Tibetan Border Police were also trapped. They had reached the summit during the blizzard, then lost their lives as they sought to descend.

In the space of 36 hours, eight people had died on Everest's slopes. It was the worst single loss of life ever to occur on the mountain.

Professional guides and mountaineers hope that those deaths will not have been in vain, that perhaps they will serve to revise the climbing tactics of future expeditions.

For example, the Hall and Fischer groups would have benefited from more careful planning concerning the setting of the fixed ropes. Not having the ropes in place resulted in costly delays. The need to carry more oxygen was another lesson to be learned.

There is an unwritten rule that no one should be on Everest's summit after two o'clock in the afternoon. This is to avoid the bad weather that comes sweeping in later in the afternoon. But Hall himself broke the rule and permitted some of his clients to do so.

Tragedy was the result. Professionals now agree that climbers must stick to a strict turnaround rule, even if it means turning back within a stone's throw of the summit.

But mostly, it is a matter of holding Everest in respect. Seventy-seven-year-old Sir Edmund Hillary, speaking from his home in Auckland, New Zealand, to a *Time* magazine correspondent, put it in these terms: "I have a feeling that people have been getting a little too casual with Mount Everest. This incident will bring them to regard it rather more seriously."

· 6 ·
Stowaway

Seventeen-year-old Armando Socarras Ramírez hated life in Cuba. He had little freedom and no opportunities.

Fidel Castro, the Cuban dictator, ruled the country with an iron hand. Hundreds of thousands of Cubans had left the country because of their opposition to Castro.

When Armando was 16, he was sent to school far from his home to learn to be a welder. But he got little training in the trade, for he was forced to spend most of his time in the fields cutting sugarcane.

Realizing that there was no future for him in Cuba, Armando began dreaming of fleeing to the United States. He had the name of an uncle who lived in New Jersey. Perhaps that uncle could help him realize his dream.

There was a big problem, however. Castro allowed only a tiny number of Cubans to leave the country. In fact, only two planes a day flew to the United States. Tens of thousands of Cubans were waiting to be booked on those two planes. It would take years before Armando could get a seat.

A friend of Armando's, Jorge Pérez Blanco, shared Armando's feelings about Cuba and life there. Jorge also thought about escaping his native land for the United States.

One day, Armando, now 22, and Jorge, 23, went to the airport in Havana, Cuba's capital, to watch the planes land and take off. When a huge jetliner bound for Spain left the ground and soared over their heads, its wheels still down, the young men looked up and saw inside the wheel wells, the spacious compartments that held the wheels once they were raised.

Suddenly, Armando had a crazy idea. Why not hide in the wheel wells of a jetliner and fly to Spain? From there, they should be able to make their way to the United States without too much trouble.

After several days of planning, Armando and Jorge were ready to put their scheme into action. The date was June 4, 1969.

At the Havana airport, Armando and Jorge hid in the grass near the end of the runway where they had seen the jetliner bound for Spain. They waited as a silvery DC-8 made its way from the terminal along a taxiway. At the end of the taxiway, the air-

Armando hid himself in the wheel well of a Douglas DC-8 just before it took off. (Wide World)

craft turned onto the runway and stopped. IBERIA AIRLINES OF SPAIN was blazoned on the plane's fuselage.

Armando and Jorge left their hiding places and raced to the aircraft. With the high-pitched scream of the jet's engines ringing in his ears, Armando climbed up the right wheel and into the wheel well. Jorge scrambled into the left one.

Inside, the wheel well was a maze of pipes, hoses, and cables. Armando crammed himself into the compartment as far as he could go.

The jet began moving down the runway, slowly at first, then gathering speed. Armando held on tight. Peering down, he could see the runway sweeping past.

The huge plane eased into the sky and began climbing. Now the ocean was beneath Armando.

Suddenly, a motor began to hum and the pipes and cables inside the wheel well started moving. The wheels were being raised.

Armando looked down to see a pair of enormous tires coming toward him. Afraid of being crushed, he squeezed himself deeper and deeper into the compartment. The wheels kept coming. Armando couldn't go any farther. Finally, the wheels stopped. Armando breathed a great sigh of relief.

On the flight deck, the pilot, Valentín Vara del Rey, noticed a red light flickering on a control panel, indicating the wheels were still down. But

Vara del Rey knew they were not. He radioed the Havana airport to say that he was going to let the wheels down and then retract them again.

Armando was beginning to get used to the darkness and his cramped quarters when suddenly the doors to the wheel well swung open and the wheels began moving away from him. Armando had no idea what was happening. Had he and Jorge been discovered? Was the plane returning to Havana? Armando looked down expecting to see the runway again, but all he saw was water.

The wheels had been down for only a second or two when they started coming up again. Once they were in place and the doors had folded shut, Armando was alone in the dark again.

On the flight deck, the pilot scanned the controls. The red light did not come back on, meaning that the wheels had been retracted successfully. With the problem solved, Pilot Vara del Rey pointed the plane for Madrid and began climbing to a cruising altitude of 29,000 feet.

As the plane ascended, the air got thin and became very cold. The temperature outside Armando's wheel well dropped to below zero and kept dropping. Dressed only in a light shirt and thin pants, Armando shivered.

As the plane kept climbing, the outside temperature kept plunging until it was 40 degrees below zero. Armando was colder than he had ever been in his life. His fingers and toes throbbed with pain. His ears ached. When he exhaled, the warm air from his nose and mouth froze and coated his face with frost.

Armando also began to feel dizzy from a lack of oxygen. Before long, Armando blacked out.

The plane sped toward Madrid with its 143 passengers, a crew of nine — and the two young stowaways. Armando awakened once during the nine-hour flight but quickly slipped back into a coma.

As the DC-8 approached the airport in Madrid, Pilot Vara del Rey lowered the wheels. Still unconscious, Armando was unaware that the flight was nearing its end. Fortunately, his body had become caught in the tangle of pipes and cables and did not fall out when the doors of the wheel well swung open.

Armando was also blessed by the fact that the pilot made a perfect landing, putting the big plane down on the runway without the slightest jolt. A hard landing might have flung Armando out onto the runway.

After the pilot taxied to the terminal, baggage handlers and mechanics approached the aircraft. One of the mechanics saw something drop from the right wheel well and land with a thud on the concrete. It was a body. "Look!" he shouted. "It's a man!"

It was Armando, his clothes and face covered with frost. He did not move. When the mechanic reached down and touched him, Armando moaned.

As Pilot Vara del Rey was leaving the plane, he heard men shouting. He walked over to see what was going on. A mechanic told him that the young man lying on the ground had stowed away in the wheel well and had been trapped there during the flight. Then Vara del Rey realized that it must have been the boy in the wheel well that caused the red light to flash after takeoff.

Someone called an ambulance and Armando was rushed to a hospital, where he quickly regained consciousness. When he arrived at the hospital, Armando's body temperature was 93 degrees, nearly six degrees below normal. Nevertheless, except for frostbitten fingers and toes, Armando seemed to be in good condition.

Armando asked about his friend Jorge. No one had an answer for him. It is believed that Jorge fell from the aircraft as the plane began its descent toward Madrid.

Spanish newspaper photographers were permitted to take photographs of Armando during his stay in the hospital. A reporter who sought to speak to him said that Armando seemed dazed and confused. But after a few days in the hospital, Armando was feeling fine.

Aviation experts were astounded that Armando had managed to survive. Dr. Charles Glasgow, chief engineer for Douglas Aircraft Company, makers of the DC-8, called Armando's survival a miracle. He couldn't understand why Armando had not been crushed to death when the big double wheel was folded into the wheel well.

Medical experts were also baffled. How had Armando managed to survive temperatures of 40 de-

Armando Ramírez gets treated for frozen fingers at a Madrid hospital. (Wide World)

grees below zero and an acute shortage of oxygen for so long a period?

Later, doctors judged that Armando's body may have entered an inactive, sleeplike state during his journey. It was similar to hibernation, the deep sleep that some animals enter during the winter.

The body temperature of hibernating animals is lower than normal. Their heartbeat rate takes a sharp drop. Chipmunks, hamsters, and squirrels are among the animals that hibernate.

Dr. Duane Catterson, a space medicine expert for the National Aeronautics and Space Administration (NASA), said that Armando may have been able to attain a state similar to hibernation because he got cold gradually.

Said Dr. Catterson to *The New York Times*: "He may have had the lucky coincidence of the right temperature drop — not enough to freeze him but enough to reduce his oxygen requirement so he could survive in that atmosphere.

"If he had been chilled too fast, it would have been fatal, but through gradual cooling his body's demand for oxygen could have kept up with the supply."

Dr. Catterson pointed out that gradual cooling was possible because of conditions inside the wheel well. The compartment was probably warm at the start of the flight because of heat from the tires and brakes. It took a fair amount of time for the compartment to get really cold.

Armando's feat, Dr. Catterson said, demonstrated the body's ability to survive in extremes and "defeat . . . Mother Nature's design." Nevertheless, he added with a grin, riding in a jet's wheel compartment is "not likely to become a popular way of travel."

As for Armando himself, he was less concerned with his health than his freedom. "Please don't send me back to Cuba," he pleaded during his hospital stay. He explained that he opposed the political system in Cuba and wanted to go to the United States. "I have an uncle living in New Jersey," Armando said, "and maybe he will help me."

Armando was able to realize his dream. In July 1969, Armando was brought to the United States under the sponsorship of the International Rescue Committee. At Kennedy Airport in New York, Armando was tearfully welcomed by his uncle, Elio Fernández of Passaic, New Jersey.

At an airport press conference, Armando, speaking of Cuba, said, "There was no future there at all for me. I was looking for a new world and a new future.

"If I was in the same situation, I would do it again."

In the years immediately following Armando's escape from Cuba, others attempted to stow away in the wheel wells of jet airliners — with tragic results.

In February 1970, some eight months after Armando's headline-making adventure, 14-year-old

Keith Sapsford hid in the wheel well of a Japanese Airline's DC-8 bound for Tokyo from Sydney, Australia. The young man fell to his death as the plane was taking off.

In mid-April 1972, John J. Gribowski, a 19-year-old U.S. Marine, stowed away in the wheel well of a Boeing 707 operated by American Airlines on a flight from San Diego to New York. Not long after the huge jet had landed at Kennedy Airport in New York, airline maintenance personnel found Gribowski's body. He had frozen to death.

After news of Armando Socarras Ramírez's survival reached the Douglas Aircraft Company, Dr. Charles Glasgow said that a person stowing away in the wheel well of a DC-8 had only "one chance in a million" of remaining alive. Nothing has happened since to change those odds.

Index

SCHOLASTIC BIOGRAPHY

❏ MP45877-9	Ann M. Martin: The Story of the Author of The Baby-sitters Club	$3.99
❏ MP44767-X	The First Woman Doctor	$3.99
❏ MP43628-7	Freedom Train: The Story of Harriet Tubman	$3.99
❏ MP42402-5	Harry Houdini: Master of Magic	$3.50
❏ MP42404-1	Helen Keller	$3.50
❏ MP44652-5	Helen Keller's Teacher	$3.99
❏ MP44818-8	Invincible Louisa	$3.50
❏ MP42395-9	Jesse Jackson: A Biography	$3.25
❏ MP43503-5	Jim Abbott: Against All Odds	$2.99
❏ MP41159-4	Lost Star: The Story of Amelia Earhart	$3.50
❏ MP44350-X	Louis Braille, The Boy Who Invented Books for the Blind	$3.50
❏ MP48109-6	Malcolm X: By Any Means Necessary	$4.50
❏ MP65174-9	Michael Jordan	$3.50
❏ MP44154-X	Nelson Mandela "No Easy Walk to Freedom"	$3.50
❏ MP42897-7	One More River to Cross: The Stories of Twelve Black Americans	$4.50
❏ MP43052-1	The Secret Soldier: The Story of Deborah Sampson	$2.99
❏ MP44691-6	Sojourner Truth: Ain't I a Woman?	$3.99
❏ MP42560-9	Stealing Home: A Story of Jackie Robinson	$3.99
❏ MP42403-3	The Story of Thomas Alva Edison, Inventor: The Wizard of Menlo Park	$3.50
❏ MP44212-0	Wanted Dead or Alive: The True Story of Harriet Tubman	$3.99
❏ MP42904-3	The Wright Brothers at Kitty Hawk	$3.99

Available wherever you buy books, or use this order form.

Scholastic Inc., P.O. Box 7502, 2931 East McCarty Street, Jefferson City, MO 65102

Please send me the books I have checked above. I am enclosing $_____ (please add $2.00 to cover shipping and handling). Send check or money order — no cash or C.O.D.s please.

Name_____ Birthdate _____

Address_____

City_____ State/Zip _____

Please allow four to six weeks for delivery. Available in the U.S. only. Sorry, mail orders are not available to residents of Canada. Prices subject to change.   BIO997